AFFIRMING CATHOLICISM

Mark D. Chapman

LITURGY, SOCIALISM AND LIFE: THE LEGACY OF CONRAD NOEL

Series Editor: Mark D. Chapman

DARTON LONGMAN + TODD

First published in 2001 by
Darton, Longman and Todd Ltd
1 Spencer Court
140–142 Wandsworth High Street
London SW18 4JJ

in association with

Affirming Catholicism
St Luke's Centre
90 Central Street
London EC1V 8AQ

ISBN 0–232–52417–3

The views expressed in this book are those of the author
and do not necessarily reflect any policy of
Affirming Catholicism.

Designed by Sandie Boccacci
Phototypeset in 10/13pt Times by Intype London Ltd
Printed and bound in Great Britain by
Page Bros, Norwich, Norfolk

Affirming Catholicism

Affirming Catholicism is a movement (not an ecclesiastical party) which exists to do two things. We affirm our
confidence in our Anglican heritage; and we seek to
renew and promote the Catholic tradition within it. Our
aim is to explore, explain and share with others both
inside and outside the Church a lively, intelligent and
inclusive Catholic faith. In the words of our Trust Deed:

> It is the conviction of many that a respect for scholar-
> ship and free enquiry has been characteristic of the
> Church of England and of the Churches of the wider
> Anglican Communion from earliest times, and is fully
> consistent with the status of those Churches as part of
> the Holy Catholic Church. It is desired to establish a
> charitable educational foundation which will be true
> both to those characteristics and to the Catholic tra-
> dition within Anglicanism...The object of the
> foundation shall be the advancement of education in
> the doctrines and the historical development of the
> Church of England and the Churches of the wider Ang-
> lican Communion, as held by those standing within the
> Catholic tradition.

Our Publications

These are offered as one means of presenting Anglican
Catholic teaching and practice in as clear and accessible
a form as possible. Some cover traditional doctrinal and
liturgical themes: others attempt to present a well-argued

Catholic viewpoint on issues of debate currently facing the Church. There is a list of our series of booklets on page v.

To order these publications individually or on subscription, or for further information about the aims and activities of Affirming Catholicism, write to:

The Secretary
Affirming Catholicism
St Luke's Centre
90 Central Street
London EC1V 8AQ

Tel: 020 7253 1138
Fax: 020 7253 1139

Books in the Affirming Catholicism series

Contents

Introduction

In his 1919 lectures on Christian socialism, Charles Raven noted that

> [w]hen the cry of the oppressed was ringing in men's ears and when Christians might have listened to the prophets of social righteousness or the victims of social evil, fifty years were wasted in lawsuits over 'regeneration' and ritual, vestments and incense and the precise meaning of sixteenth-century values. In Christ's time also there were some who were so earnest about the washing of the chalice and paten and the tithing of mint and anise and cummin that they neglected justice and mercy and faith.[1]

The intervening eighty years may have seen the subjects of the ecclesiastical debate change, but it is not clear to me that the Church of England – at least in its official bodies – is any more ready to listen to the voices from the margins or the new social prophets. Revising the liturgy as a panacea for social disengagement might still be the order of the day, but there is little evidence that the ideals of 'sacramental socialism'[2] espoused earlier in the century have made much contribution to the debate. Its emphasis on the integration of liturgy and society seems to have been lost in the consumerist religion of the late twentieth century.

For so many of the great liberal catholics of the past, however, worship did not exist in another world, it was not concerned with carving out a little bit of heaven on earth, but was instead about giving the best from this world, the best of human creativity, back to God. And that meant it was a way of drawing together two worlds – the redeemed world with its beauty and enormous potential for good, and the heavenly world where all would see beauty face to face. Consequently, to use the products of human sin and injustice in the service of God was pure hypocrisy. This had two effects: it demanded beauty in everything, both in the Church and outside. But it also meant that questions had to be asked – about what mars the beauty of the earth and of our fellow humanity. Could something be beautiful if it was produced under sweated conditions? For sacramental socialists, good liturgy demanded a just world. The diatribes of one of its pioneers, Percy Dearmer, were to be taken to heart. He wrote in the introduction to *The Parson's Handbook*:

> It has been pointed out that a modern preacher often stands in a sweated pulpit, wearing a sweated surplice over a suit of clothes that were not produced under fair conditions, and, holding a sweated book in one hand, with the other he points to the machine-made cross at the jerry-

built altar, and appeals to the sacred principles of mutual sacrifice and love.[3]

Such an integrated approach to liturgy and the world might be far removed from the often escapist sentimentalism of much modern Anglican worship, but it provided a powerful influence on one of the most eccentric, dynamic and radical parish priests of the twentieth century: Conrad le Despencer Roden Noel, for most of his career Vicar of Thaxted in North-west Essex. For Noel, socialism, catholicism, beauty and duty were combined in a vision, often tinged with humour, of a church capable of transforming the world but never out of touch with that world. This can be clearly seen from an advertisement for the post of curate which Noel placed in the *Church Times*, the leading Anglo-Catholic newspaper, towards the end of 1918. It read as follows:

> Missionary work in England. Priest wanted for some months or permanent. In general sympathy with manifesto of Catholic Crusade, and with decisions of the Catholic reforming Councils versus Papal Autocracy of all kinds. Piety preferred to pietism; no quarter given to moderation and safety. Hard, uphill work; no worldly advantages. Graduate not necessary. For 'society' the comradeship of the poor. Salary poor owing to absence of official grants £180. Healthy, active revolutionary; good singing voice.[4]

Seldom, if ever, have the terms 'active revolutionary' and 'good singing voice' been juxtaposed as qualities desirable in one and the same person. And yet, in some ways, these are the qualities that describe the Vicar of Thaxted himself, as he sought to unite the demands of joyful and popular worship with a social gospel. Noel was a special kind of catholic and a special kind of socialist who was able to leave his mark on a Church which, because of the antiquated splendours of freehold and private patronage, had space for the eccentric and the original. By looking at Noel's writings, as well as some of the more controversial episodes in his life, this booklet seeks to illustrate his peculiarly appealing brand of catholic socialism, which combines a romantic English nationalism with a deeper internationalism, both of which are rooted in a vision of catholicity, worship and wholeness. It seems to me that his integrated vision, though undoubtedly deeply flawed and often naïve, has lessons for the future of English catholic socialism in our own day. After all, like the Christian religion, socialism has seldom been practised with a sufficient sense of joy and self-irony.

1. Early Career

Noel was born into an aristocratic family on 12 July 1869, a grandson of the Earl of Gainsborough and son of a Groom in the privy chamber. His father, Roden Noel, a notorious bisexual, had, however, relinquished his post after discovering radicalism, and eventually came to write the English words to the Red Flag. His mother, Alice de Broe, was the daughter of a Swiss banker and a convinced evangelical. Noel was educated under the tyrannical Edward White Benson (who went on to become the Archbishop of Canterbury) at Wellington and afterwards moved to Cheltenham. He went up to Corpus Christi College in Cambridge, but failed to complete his course on account of (as he later claimed) an over-zealous taste for beer. It was at Cambridge that he met his future wife Miriam, who later shared in his project of popular theology. Despite not gaining his degree he went on to Chichester Theological College, which marked the beginnings of his somewhat idiosyncratic brand of socialist Anglo-Catholicism. He wrote later of this time in his book, *Jesus the Heretic*:

> I remember that at my theological College . . . I used to pin up on my walls startling sayings [on

equality etc], together with the sayings of the early Catholic Fathers ... Students who considered themselves 'correct catholic' of unimpeachable orthodoxy would scoff at these 'monstrous' and 'subversive' slogans; and I would then politely ask them to unfold the authors' names, and they were embarrassed to find themselves confronted with names such as those of Tertullian, Ambrose [etc] ... Whether I converted many by this means I am uncertain, but it is a form of propaganda which I would recommend to my younger student friends with a sense of fun and mischief.[5]

Here, as with so much of Noel's work, there is a great sense of fun, a general assault on priggishness and puritanism in all senses of the word, as well as a distancing from the overly-precise prissy ritualism and mimicry of Rome which had developed by the end of the nineteenth century out of some strands of Anglo-Catholicism. It may be 'necessary to point out,' Noel wrote in *The Life of Jesus*, 'that conventionality and orthodoxy are completely different matters, and that many who boast the name of Catholic would be surprised and shocked at what the tradition actually involves'.[6]

Despite his taste for ceremonial and beauty, Noel's own brand of catholicism seems to have been much more influenced by F.D. Maurice's understanding of the Church as the spiritual dimension of the nation, and, at least potentially, comprising all people, than by Pusey and his successors who formed a spiritual huddle of those who claimed to possess the whole truth. Like Maurice, Noel believed in what he called a 'democratic catholic' theology. 'Clumsy critics,' he wrote in *Socialism in Church History*,

> ... will always describe Maurice and Kingsley as broad Churchmen, but in fact they protested against broad Churchism as being almost as anti-Christian as Puseyism or popular Protestantism. Their lives were devoted to the revival of Catholic democratic Faith. Maurice was a profoundly original Catholic theologian, not bound by the letter of tradition, but developing its spirit.[7]

Indeed throughout his life one of Noel's objects of attack was what he called 'sectarianism', by which he meant any form of ecclesiastical sectionalism, and anything that did not point beyond itself towards a universalism and internationalism. Thus he wrote in a collection of essays published in 1912:

> Puseyism and Papalism have been too sectarian. They have partly devised or kept alive the Catholic idea, but they have not preached the Catholic Faith in its proportion and fullness. But just in the measure that the *democracy* becomes really Catholic will the Catholic Truth which lurks behind its partial expression by the various Christian bodies clear the issues ... The true and lifeless thing that men now call Christianity leads

not only bad men but good men, to revolt. The Catholic Faith preached in all its reasonableness will draw all men into it, or at least all men of goodwill. Nowadays the Faith is preached in so distorted a form as to drive the sheep from the fold and leave the goats placidly browsing inside.[8]

This points towards a sense of catholicity as the expression of popular religiosity rooted in democracy and equality, but also in the revitalisation of the traditions which unite doctrine and practice. Indeed, throughout his life, Noel was less interested in right belief than in right action: there could be no right belief which did not issue in right practice. Once again life in the world and the Church had to be seen as one.

2. Ordination and Early Socialism

Noel's first great brush with the authorities came on the morning of his ordination: he was to be placed in an advanced ritualist church of Romanist persuasion, All Saints' in Plymouth. However, the Bishop of Exeter, E. H. Bickersteth, summoned him to his rooms and told him: 'I have been wrestling with the Lord in prayer all night, and it would be dangerous for you to go to All Saints.' Noel remarked of this episode in his *Autobiography*:

> I pointed out to him that he had already accepted me, and although I loved the service at All Saints', I by no means shared all Fr. Chase's views. 'Ah, that's the trouble', he said, 'for you add to his Romanism your own Pantheism, and you must know that Pantheism is a heresy'.[9]

It took him some time before he eventually found ordination; his father wrote to various bishops and even the socialist Westcott in Durham refused. During this period of waiting Noel spent much time studying living conditions. On one occasion he turned up at Percy Dearmer's house dressed as a tramp while living at Rowton House, Vauxhall, the 'working man's hotel'.[10] However, he was finally ordained in 1894 in the Chester diocese, although his advocacy of socialism and his fraternising with non-conformists prevented him from taking up his post. Nevertheless he eventually found a curacy in Salford with Edward Lee Hicks, who later became Bishop of Lincoln, after some special pleading by Charles Gore.[11]

Throughout this time Noel was active in the socialist Guild of St Matthew (which never included more than 364 among its membership) which had been founded by the radical Anglo-Catholic, Stewart Headlam, and flourished in the late 1880s and early 1890s.[12] Like Noel, Headlam was something of a liberal in theology, and they both shared a hatred of puritanism. Headlam introduced Noel to the ballet, and encouraged him in his ministry to the public houses and theatres of London, about which Noel later became passionate. With regard to the public house, he wrote in a fascinating essay entitled 'The Heresy of the Teetotallers':

> Undesirable as are many features of the English public-house, if we could only get an English bishop to spend an occasional evening in an English tavern, not with the object of 'doing good' but of enjoying himself, I believe his testimony would be of real value to the temperate and of no value to the teetotaller. In spite of all defects, the tavern possesses none of the exclusiveness of the private club, but is for all sorts and conditions of men.[13]

It was this sense of inclusiveness and democracy that characterised both Noel's socialism as well as his theology. Not surprisingly Noel, a confirmed *bon viveur*, did not see eye to eye with his incumbent, Hicks, a strict teetotaller. Hicks' biographer suggests that Noel was 'more interested in the stage, good restaurants and socialist meetings . . . than the poor of Salford'.[14]

After two years in Salford, Noel went to St Philip's, Newcastle (where helpfully his cousin, Dr Jacob was the bishop) working with Fr W.E. Moll, who was already famous as a socialist. Here he began his lifelong friendship with his fellow assistant priest, Percy Widdrington, who became an incumbent in Coventry and a prominent socialist Christian, later moving to Great Easton in Essex in 1918. In Newcastle Noel engaged in an active preaching ministry, campaigning vigorously for socialism. He soon drew many critics: at one point, for instance, he had spoken at a spiritualist meeting which caused consternation among his fellow clergy, who sent a round robin letter of protest to the bishop. Instead of replying, the bishop threw it straight in the waste bin.[15] On another occasion, during the Boer War, Noel had preached a strongly anti-war sermon which provoked some of his congregation, many of whom worked in the munitions industry, to come out against him. One threatened to blow up the church unless Noel was banned from preaching. His vicar responded: 'By all means let it go on as it is the truth, and if we lose our church, which is the ugliest structure in Newcastle, we can build a new one with the insurance money.'[16]

After two years Noel returned to London where he worked at St Mary's, Paddington Green under A.L. Lilley, who was a great friend of several of the leading Roman Catholic Modernists. Here he became a close friend with the Chesterton brothers, as well as Charles Masterman, the liberal journalist. In 1904 he joined his friend, Percy Dearmer, at St Mary's, Primrose Hill, as half-time curate. Dearmer was one of the most influential of liberal Anglo-Catholic priests and was instrumental in the production of the *English Hymnal*, itself something of a manifesto for sacramental socialism,[17] as well as in the revitalisation of English patterns of worship in distinction from the Romanising tendencies of the Society of SS Peter and Paul. The pageantry and dignity of worship, as well as the love of plainchant, were shared by Noel, although he had little of Dearmer's reverence for the second year of the reign of Edward VI or the so-called British Museum religion. Comparing the two men, Sydney Dark, editor of Noel's *Autobiography*, wrote: 'Even in his eccentricities, Dearmer was always correct; Conrad was the born iconoclast, with a never-failing impish delight in outraging convention and upsetting the respectable.'[18]

By 1906 the organised socialism of the Church of England was at a relatively low ebb at precisely the same time as the secular socialists were beginning to make headway in parliament; and it was out of what remained of the Guild of St Matthew that a group of socialists formed a new organisation, the Church Socialist League, which was far more explicitly socialist and less fixated than the Guild on the single issue of land reform.[19] From 1908 Noel became its full-time organising secretary, living in a timber-framed house in Coggeshall in Essex provided by his brewer friend, Buxton. In his *Autobiography*, Noel wrote of the aims of the League:

> Its basis was the belief that the Catholic Faith, as held and taught by the Church of England, finds its expression and application on the economic side in a Christian Socialism, which is not, as some appear to think, a particular variety of Socialism, milder than the secular brand, but economic Socialism come to by the road of the Christian Faith and inspired by the ideas of the Gospel.[20]

The approach of the CSL was more specifically partisan than most Christian social organisations, particularly Henry Scott Holland's Christian Social Union:

> The CSL consists of Church people who accept the principles of socialism, viz.: The political, economic and social emancipation of the whole people, men and women, by the establishment of a democratic commonwealth in which the

community shall own the land and capital collectively and use them for the good of all.[21]

Once again the key notions of democracy and commonwealth provide the main thrust of Noel's brand of socialism, and betray the powerful influence of F.D. Maurice. In an essay on why Catholics should be socialists, Noel stresses the solidarity of all people and the need to work together to form a 'Co-operative Commonwealth'.[22]

However, there was something far more dynamic and revolutionary in Noel than in Maurice, the former deriving his battle cry from the Magnificat: 'if the phrases had not become so well worn and meaningless,' he wrote, it 'would strike the same idlers as more revolutionary than the Marseillaise.'[23] In *The Life of Jesus*, written towards the end of his life, this becomes clearer: Noel points to his 'incalculable' debt to Lenin,[24] but he sees him as inconsistent in classifying all Christianity as 'poisonous and reactionary'. Noel agreed with Marx that religion could easily become 'the opium of the people' but he did not see this as a necessity, and he reminded his readers of what Charles Kingsley had also written in 1848:

> We have never told you that the ... true poor man's book, the true God's voice against tyrants, idlers, and humbugs, was the Bible. Ay, you may sneer, but so it is. It is our fault, our great fault, that you should sneer, sneer at the only news that ought to be your glory and your strength. It is

our fault. We have used the Bible as if it were a special constable's handbook – *an opium dose for keeping beasts of burden patient while they were being overloaded* – a mere book to keep the poor in order.[25]

For Noel, there was a revolutionary and anti-establishment character to socialism, which although usually swamped by the forces of plutocracy, manifested itself at crucial moments through the history of the Church. And it was this revolutionary form of Christianity that was revived in 'such modern bodies as the Church Socialist League, the Catholic Crusade, and the Order of the Church Militant . . .[This] was no mere eccentricity, but is inspired by Holy Scripture and the most living of the Church's traditions'.[26] 'Why,' Noel asked at the end of the same book, 'has the revolutionary zeal died down onto comfortable complacency? What has stifled the laughter?'[27]

Noel's style of socialism was neither doctrinaire nor naïve.[28] As Edward Norman suggests, 'although Noel can easily be written off as an upper-class "folk" romantic, addicted to Morris dancing and flying the red flag from the tower of his church, this would do his intelligence a considerable injustice. He was a critical thinker, whose socialism, despite its peculiarities, had impressive qualities.'[29] This judgement is borne out in Noel's first substantial book, his history of Christian socialism, *Socialism in Church History*, published in 1910.

Although his historical analysis is derivative, his discussion of current trends is perceptive and incisive, especially in relation to the Christian Social Union, that broad alliance of Anglican churchmen interested in social thought. The 'danger of Social-Unionism,' he claimed, 'is that its leaders, arriving at no clear dogma in theology or politics, and being for the most part political un-denominationalists, have no fixed standard by which to judge the value or otherwise of any suggested social reform.'[30] And although Noel did not wish to tie the churches to any one political party, he was quite clear that socialism resulted in a set of values which functioned as an *absolute* standard for moral decisions: 'the philosophy of socialism is fellowship, justice among men, the value of the *whole* of life, material, mental, spiritual.[31] While admitting that the 'Christian Faith cannot be summed up in the word socialism, nor should it be finally identified with any political system,' Noel nevertheless claimed that 'Churchmen are convinced that the principles which underlie socialism are, as far as they go, the principles of the Christian religion as applied to political, commercial and industrial problems'.[32]

This sense of wholeness and integration between the spiritual and the material, between God and the world, led him to criticise both secular socialism as well as exclusivist strands of Anglo-Catholicism and Evangelicalism. Indeed he suggests that the two heresies had strong parallels to one another:

'Calvin and Pusey believed in God and not in Man. Marx ... believed in Man and not in God. Many High Churchmen believe in original sin but not in original righteousness. Many atheists believe in original righteousness but not in original sin.' Noel goes on, however, to observe a possible gradual convergence between different ecclesiastical groups as they began to view life from an integrated socialist angle. Indeed he continues (somewhat implausibly): 'The socialist movement is bringing all these forces together on a common platform, and in our own day we see the catholic church in its Embryo stage'.[33] With regard to the Church of England, Noel believed (perhaps more plausibly) that

> ... her own peculiar position should help her towards socialism. The socialist is anti-imperialist and anti-competitive in the economic sphere. Is that not precisely the attitude of the English Church in the religious sphere? She criticizes and repudiates the imperialism of Rome and the competitive theories of dissenters. Her ideal is one of national churches, but these national churches are not to be insular and self-sufficient; they are but democratically governed provinces of the International or Catholic Church of God.[34]

As will become clear, this theme of internationalism and co-operation, together with the attack on imperialism, characterised Noel's socialism throughout his life.

3. Early Thaxted Days

In 1910 Noel was offered the living of Thaxted Church by Frances Evelyn, Countess of Warwick, an erstwhile mistress of Edward VII. At first sight she was a somewhat surprising benefactor and patron. She had, however, been converted to socialism after a ball at Warwick Castle which had been criticised in a local socialist newspaper as wasteful and extravagant; by 1906 she was contributing large sums to the Social Democratic Federation, the most Marxist of the groups which formed the early Labour party. She was also keen on ensuring that socialists were placed in her collection of Essex livings, and, before appointing Noel, she had already appointed Ernest Maxted to the nearby parish of Great Easton: he at once reformed the worship in a catholic direction and preached unmitigated socialism.

Noel was inducted on 21 September 1910, and was provided with a curate and a secretary by his patron, who had intended him to use Thaxted as a base to ensure him a reasonable income, so that he could pursue his socialist activities throughout the country. Almost from the first day, however, he devoted a great deal of energy to reforming the life of the parish church, instituting a sung eucharist at 9.00 a.m. as the main Sunday service. His first great battle was over the Bible boxes which were used by the richer parishioners to reserve their places in church, and which deprived many of the poorer members of the congregation of the best seats. This caused consternation among some of the wealthier parishioners and resignations were offered. Unlike most people, however, Noel was prepared to accept resignations, and within a couple of years he had managed to sack the organist and most of the members of the surpliced choir. At the same time he developed a new mixed choir located at the west end of the church thereby liberating himself from one of the worst products of the ecclesiological movement. Change was rapid: by Easter of 1911 he had introduced incense into worship and the parish communion had replaced matins as the main act of Sunday worship.

Miriam, who was a skilled needlewoman, provided the church with new banners and vestments, and at the same time a number of Victorian accretions were removed: 'To beautify a church,' Noel once said, 'take things out of it.' He was keen on keeping feasts and introduced processions on almost every possible occasion. In a retrospective passage in his *Autobiography* which points to the connections between ceremony and his vision of the kingdom, he wrote:

> Now what is there in the Thaxted worship which scandalizes the 'ratepayer' and attracts many in

the town itself and many pilgrims from all quarters? Perhaps it is the homeliness and unconventionality which many people appreciate. The organ and the surpliced choir no longer predominate. The processions on High Days and Holidays include not only the ceremonial group in bright vestments but the people themselves, children with flowers and branches, women in gay veils, men with torches and banners, all this movement centering round the Lord Christ present in the Eucharist. We preach the Christ who all through His life stressed the value of the common meal, the bread and the wine joyously shared among His people, the Mass as prelude to the New World Order in which all would be justly produced and equally distributed. The Lord thus chose the ordinary things of everyday life, the useful bread and the genial wine, to be the perpetual vehicles of His presence among us till His kingdom should come on earth as in Heaven. But all this involves politics, and we are often rebuked for mixing politics with religion. Well! The blind following of any political party, the politics of the party hack, these are certainly not the business of the pulpit; but politics in the wider sense of social justice, are part and parcel of the Gospel of Christ, and to ignore them is to be false to His teaching. Worship and beauty are not to be despised, but worship divorced from social righteousness is an abomination to God.[35]

Beauty and popular participation or what he called 'triumphant gaiety', and which he regarded as the hallmark of the early Christians,[36] thus became an expression of democracy in worship as a prelude to the kingdom of God as the church became a pointer to the New World Order. As John Milbank has written: 'The joy of Thaxted was a wise joy. The liturgy and the music and the dancing were as essential to Christian socialism as work amongst the poor.'[37] Noel himself confirmed this judgement later in his life during the period of the Catholic Crusade in an unpublished set of sermon notes:

> The Crusade is not merely concerned with politics and economics, nor could it possibly be so if it is a Catholic society, any more than it could claim the name of Catholic if it were not, among other things, directly concerned with politics and economics. We, therefore, consider it essential, as Christians, to attack falsity and shoddiness in the literature, music, architecture, and other arts, of the Church and Nation. We regard this as an essential part of the political fight.[38]

This integrated approach is demonstrated in Noel's enthusiasm for processions, which also expresses something of his understanding of the physicality of the presence of Christ, pointing to the materiality of the incarnation and the redemption of nature. And yet such processions provoked some of the more extreme Protestants of his own Church, who were organised into 'Kensit's Wycliffe

Preachers'. One particular occasion for protest was the ninth midsummer festival, which was to include a procession of the blessed sacrament, and which was to be as colourful as any ever seen in Thaxted. The Bishop of Chelmsford, a staunch Evangelical, was far from keen on the idea and telegrammed his disfavour to Noel:

> Just heard that you intend to carry the Host through the streets today. Can scarcely imagine this correct, but if it is, I, as your father in God, absolutely prohibit the same either inside or outside your church. Shall be glad of a telegram that rumour is incorrect. God bless and Guide you.[39]

Noel used this episcopal snub to good effect, pointing out that he had received an episcopal blessing, since he was going to process inside *and* outside the church. Needless to say, he refused to obey his bishop; at the end of the day, when the leader of the Kensitites had discovered that there was virtually no opposition to Noel in the town, he and his wife rather bemusedly accepted Noel's invitation to tea. And it was reported that he soon gave up his preaching. Noel found the Kensitite disturbances as well as their ignorance of ritualist terms altogether rather amusing. As he wrote in *Byways of Belief*:

> There is only one war of extermination which is at any time justifiable, and that is the war against

the sour bigots who spend their time in the attempt to exterminate everybody else. But, after all, are the Kensitites worth expelling? Have they not made the world a merrier place with their little jokes abut sunflowers and thurifers, which they say they have seen suspended in front of the altars in their beloved Church of England.[40]

Noel's most famous expression of the beautification of life was his deliberate revitalisation of things medieval and traditional: he introduced chapels dedicated to those he regarded as champions of the people, including John Ball, the priest who headed the Peasants' Revolt, as well as to Thomas à Becket, whom he regarded (somewhat implausibly) as a champion of the people against the state. More influential, however, was the revival of dancing as a return to English roots in an attempt to cultivate a sense of community which transcended class. It was actually his wife who organised the first visit of dancers from Miss Neale's academy; and soon the Morris was regularly being danced in Thaxted. Within a few years, Cecil Sharp, a fellow socialist and the most important collector of folk song and dance, was a frequent visitor. In relation to this, there is a rather touching piece from a catechism essay written by a disabled eight-year-old:

> Some people are graceful in body and move about gracefully and it is a pleasure to look at them. We cannot all be graceful in body, but God

wants us all to be graceful in soul. God wants
Thaxted to be a little town of people living
beautiful and graceful lives, and being generous
to each other, in honour preferring one another,
serving each other.[41]

Alongside this popular expression of dancing, there
was also a revival of church music, particularly
during the time when Gustav Holst lived in
Thaxted at weekends: he composed his *Planets*
there. He brought choirs from Morley College and
St Paul's School, and organised festivals and con-
certs with broad popular appeal (and often with a
decidedly heterodox theology).

Before long, Noel's reforms to worship and
church life spread to the wider Church through his
team of curates and disciples. One commentator,
the left-wing journalist, Kingsley Martin, remarked
about his own visit to Thaxted:

There was fun [in the Church]: . . .the congregation was expected to take part in the service.
I won't say there was nothing precious about
Thaxted. There were odd-looking men in sandals
and women in hand-woven costumes, and their
influence was to be seen in a certain artiness
in the shops. True, Conrad's disciples did dance
Morris-dances in the road, and deliberately
revive a medieval atmosphere. But the dancing
was *fun*, and if Conrad wanted to revive what
the romantics believe to have been the feeling

and the tradition of the Middle Ages, he was not unsuccessful. It would be a superficial observer who dismissed Thaxted as 'ye olde'.[42]

In a lyrical passage from the end of *The Life of Jesus*, Noel wrote of Christian joy:

Many prophets have mourned to the people, and sometimes wept, but after these necessary forerunners there seemed to have arisen One who had lured men with his shepherd's pipes and they had begun to dance. So true is this that the folk in a later age sang their creed in a ballad form under the title of 'The General Dance'.[43]

4. Mature Socialism: 'The Catholic Crusade of the Servants of the Precious Blood to Transform the Kingdom of this World into the Commonwealth of God'

As the First World War progressed and the socialist movement divided over pacifism, Noel became increasingly disillusioned with the less than radical stance of the CSL, and by 1918 he had set up the Catholic Crusade, 'a movement of Catholic Anglicans, who were socialists and would work through the Church for a new economic society basing itself on the law and principles of the gospels and the prophets'.[44] This became much more explicitly socialist and also much more explicitly Catholic than the earlier organisation, and was the first Church body to show open support for the Bolshevik Revolution of 1917. Noel's most outspoken subject was his hostility towards imperialism in general and the British Empire in particular, the aims of the Crusade being to 'shatter the British Empire and all Empires to bits, wrestling against principalities and highly-placed powers'. The Church was to be the 'nucleus of the universal

Kingdom wherein dwelleth righteousness, the midwife of a new world in the pangs of birth'.[45]

The Manifesto of the Catholic Crusade is a lengthy document which repeats many of Noel's favourite themes including liberty, fraternity and equality. These traditional revolutionary themes are coupled with the more English Romantic, arts and crafts strand of Ruskin and Morris-style socialism: there was the need to preserve the freedom to be creative, and also for every person to delight 'in his leisure, his craft, having his lot in such personal and common ownership as shall encourage initiative in fellowship'. In turn, the Crusade stood for justice and dignity, seeking to overthrow the state if it did not encourage such virtues. This was to lead to the 'resistance of Christ in God's quarrel for Commonwealth'. In short, the purpose was to create

> ... a free England in a Communion of Free Nations – a free England, in which the freedom of the redeemer, the last shall be first and the first last. In which, in the Spirit of Saint John the Herald, the valleys shall be raised and hills leveled. In which, by the prayers of St James, the workers shall rejoice that they are exalted, and the plutocrats in that they are brought low; in which, in the eager desire of Our Lady, the mighty shall be dragged from their seat, the hungry filled and the rich sent away empty. In which, in the prophecy of Saint John the

Evangelist, the traffickers in oil and wheat and the bodies of souls and men shall lament, as the smoke of their burning cities ascends to the heavens; in which, in the hope of Saint Cyprian, the essentials of life shall not be held by the few to the exclusion of the many; in which, in the teaching of Saint Ambrose, the common property of the people shall be restored and all enslaving ownership disallowed; in which, following Saint Gregory, who sent us our religion, the land shall be for the workers and none shall be owned by the shirkers.

Noel goes on in similar vein citing the rebellions of 1381, 1450 and 1549 before ending with a challenge:

We will rather mix earth and heaven together than to endure so great a cruelty. We ask of you everything; we offer you nothing – nothing but adventure, risks, battle, perhaps ruin; with the love and loyalty of comrades and the Peace of God which passeth understanding.[46]

With this revolutionary message the battle lines were drawn for the disputes of the 1920s.

At the time of the Coal Miners' Strike, shortly after the end of the First World War, when a general strike was averted, and when Randall Davidson, Archbishop of Canterbury, ordered prayers to be said in thanksgiving, a simple poem was chalked up on a blackboard outside

Thaxted Church. This proved typical of Noel's radical socialism:

The rich man's war
on the workers –
It has always been so.
The few live in comfort and folly
    By robbing the many.
    The RICH killed Jesus,
    The Poor Man's Friend
    The king, the Empire,
The rich and their toadies
      KILLED CHRIST.
Our Rulers, the Empire, the Rich,
And those who surround them
      Kill Him NOW.
Inasmuch as ye have done it unto the least
of these (the IRISH AND THE MINERS),
      Ye have done it unto Me.[47]

Although it never attracted a large following, the Catholic Crusade became influential on a number of radical priests including the young Alan Ecclestone through the mediation of Jim Wilson. Like many other socialist organisations it was to split in 1936 over the Trotsky-Stalin issue, with Noel and other members forming the vigorously anti-Stalinist Order of the Church Militant. Among its many aims was the proclamation of the 'Blessed Trinity as the Source, Sustenance and Goal of Life: striving to re-shape the World after the pattern of this social God', the creation of 'groups of people so filled with the Spirit that they should be a fore-taste and inthrust of Christ's international Commonwealth'. To this end they pledged them-selves (among other things) to 'revive all the Sacraments, especially in their forgotten social sig-nificance'.[48] Once again the vision was that of an integration of world and worship in an all-embracing new world order.

5. The Battle of the Flags

If this explicit socialism wasn't enough to outrage the more conservative population, Noel placed three flags inside the church against the chancel arch: the red flag, the flag of St George, and the Irish tricolour (which had been given during the war after the Easter rising in 1916 by a parishioner, a Mrs Griffiths, and which at the time, before the partition of Ireland, was the flag of Sinn Fein). This provoked bitter hostility in some quarters, especially amongst some Cambridge undergraduates, who removed the red flag and the Sinn Fein banner substituting in their place a Union Jack. Noel soon replaced the flags, an act of defiance which even made the front page of the *Illustrated London News*. And later he went on to burn the Union Jack.

Not surprisingly all this led to controversy with the diocesan authorities, since Noel had no faculty for the flags. Noel defended his actions in an extraordinary short book, *The Battle of the Flags*. The Bishop of Chelmsford accused Noel of disloyalty to his oath of allegiance, to which he responded: 'If the Government, yielding to the clamour of the plutocratic press, attempts to make the flags illegal, it will then become necessary to discuss the exact nature of the oath.'[49] He also pointed to the popular support for the flags in church, the new Parochial Church Council having unanimously supported Noel's action on 14 July 1921 and reaffirmed the 'Christian principles for which they stand'.[50] And it was on their suggestion that a motto was added to the red flag: 'He hath made of one blood all nations.' Noel was highly critical of the efforts to have the flags removed by the ecclesiastical courts: 'While Union Jacks are allowed without faculty in countless churches,' he wrote, 'the gross unfairness of an attack upon our flags by use of faculty will be obvious to everyone.'[51] Eventually, however, Noel was forced by law to remove the flags on the grounds that they had provoked rioting. During these proceedings he remarked to the Chancellor of the diocese: 'Well, Mr Chancellor, as your ruling was based on the Red Flag having caused rioting, supposing I stirred up some of my East End friends to riot and tear the Union Jack from their Churches, what would your judgment be then?'[52] However, before this final ruling, there was a great deal of heated controversy in the church press, in the national dailies and even as far afield as Moscow. At one point, when the vicarage was under siege, Lady Warwick's son appeared in his Rolls Royce to rescue Noel, who refused the aid. Meanwhile Noel's own force of peaceful 'police' organised by the Christian Socialist pacifist politician, George Lansbury, had slashed the tyres of the protesters.

Noel defended his use of flags with vigour, beginning with the flag of St George, the flag of England. He felt that this was the fitting national flag in distinction to the Union Jack, which had deceived the people under the influence of 'Prussian-minded Imperialists, who were anxious that they should forget the flag of old England; for financiers, politicians, and newspaper-proprietors grow fat upon Empire while they build an England fit for heroes to starve in'. The Union Jack, he went on, 'is the modern flag of brute-force dominion. In its present form it was constructed to celebrate the triumph of a swollen, greedy Empire'.[53] Noel came out strongly against anything that smacked of imperialism: 'Why should not the cry of "St George for merry England" drown the bombastic cry of St Jack for dismal Empire?'[54]

When it came to defending the Irish Tricolour, Noel continued his anti-imperialist theme, emphasising the right of self-determination, for which the First World War had supposedly been fought.[55] However, nationalism could not be seen as an end in itself: the red flag was there to serve as a pointer to something more universal than the nation. As the flag of Catholic France, as well as the flag of international socialism, it emphasised the notion of God as fellowship, and of the commonwealth and democracy of nations, none of which could be allowed to exist as an isolated entity.[56] 'In the blood-red banner of Jesus Christ, of the early and medieval Christian and of modern times, are symbolised the ideals of the group, the nation, and the international, to which we as worshippers of the One in Many and the Many in One are pledged.'[57] Jesus loved his country, according to Noel, but the Gospels

> ... suggest this interplay of nationalism and the international as essential to the building up of the World to Come. The flags of Nations and the flag of the International should therefore be lifted together as the ensigns of the Faith and Christian Nations.[58]

In short, Noel claimed, national flags would always have their place as a focus of love and loyalty, but were never sufficient because of the doctrines of '... the equality of men within the nation and the federation of the nations within a world commonwealth. The Red Flag, restoring these truths, restores the balance.'[59]

Noel was as bitterly critical of the singing of the national anthem, and of the Royal family that it represented (which has a certain irony given that he was born in a grace and favour house). In *Jesus the Heretic*, he speaks of the 1935 Jubilee and 1937 Coronation as processions before an admiring public of '... rent-lords, financiers and plutocrats of every kind. The English Monarchy is surrounded by just that host of official flunkeys and exploiters of the poor as Samuel had foretold.'[60] In turn, a Jubilee with no act of restoration was a travesty, as was the singing of Blake's 'Jerusalem' along with the national anthem, that synonym for 'God save

the System!' Indeed, according to Noel, '*Jerusalem*
contained just those "politics" and "knavish tricks"
which the national anthem was bent on frus-
trating'.[61] With rhetorical flourish, Noel asks:
' "Send her victorious", What does it mean? Victorious over the poor working conspirators; over
Prince Charlie and the Scots...."God save the
king!" ...was imposed upon the people by toadies
and court flunkeys.'[62] With typical mischief, he goes
on, remarking that, since the King no longer rules
over us, we should perhaps now be singing:

> O Lord, our God arise,
> Guard our securities,
> Don't Let them fall!
> Confound all party hacks,
> Save those my party backs,
> And let the Income tax,
> Be optional![63]

6. Doctrinal Underpinning

Noel tried to ground his blend of the national and the international, the particular and the universal, in the doctrines of the Church, emphasising most especially the Trinity in whose image the 'world-commonwealth in which the equality and justice and mercy of its divine original will be manifested'[64] as well as the material nature of the sacraments. Thus from flags Noel moves quickly to God: 'God is fellowship, or, in theological language, Trinity, and [we] believe that from everlasting God was no personal and isolated self-lover, but a community of persons bound together by natural love, justice and mercy in one being.'[65] Later in the same book, he claims:

> Variety in unity is the fundamental law for the well-being of individuals, of nations and of mankind.
>
> For Christians who have really mastered the meaning of the Faith, this conviction is strengthened by our belief in the source of our life as a Sociality, God the Trinity, the One in Many and the Many in One. We believe that there is both unity and variety in the Social Being from whom the world proceeds and in Whom the world is sustained, and that the secret of that being

is better expressed by the variety in unity of the rich chord than by the thin unity of the solitary note.[66]

This image of harmony was one of Noel's favourites. As he wrote in *Byways of Belief*: 'God is not, nor ever was, solitary, separate, alone ... God's oneness is better presented by the rich unity of the chord than by the meagre unit of the single note. God is the perfect harmony whence all proceeds and whither all things tend.'[67] He returns to this theme late in his life in *Jesus the Heretic*:

> [I]f Variety in Unity, the rich harmony of Being, be indeed our source, it is no dull world of uniformity that we shall be building, it is most accurately called the International ... In the New World Order then, there will be an infinite variety of types, of persons, of families, of nations – no longer divided and disharmonious, but expressing themselves through their different instruments in the great orchestra of God's will.[68]

In the Introduction to this book, Noel speaks of the 'Blessed Trinity as the Basis of a New World Order', looking forward to a 'world of infinite variety in harmony, of living harmony, not of dead uniformity ... It is the will of the Triune God to inspire men to renew the world in such a way as to make it the perfect expression of His own Being.'[69] Elsewhere he remarked that it was the Trinitarian doctrine of God that

... leads us to believe in nationality and the family, and, indeed, all natural family groupings, not as passing-places in the development of ill-educated peoples, who on attaining their majority will voluntarily abandon nationality for the happy mush of a smooth and undifferentiated international, but in the permanent and eternal value of variety in unity, of the many and the one.[70]

The three flags in Thaxted Church were thus, Noel concludes, 'complementary, and symbolise fundamental truths without recognition of which men must perish'.[71]

Against this Trinitarian theology, the Arians of the early Church and Individualists of the modern world could think of God only as the great distant dictator in the sky. In this context Noel attacks the Oxford Group Movement, the populist student movement led by Frank Buchman, which, he says, 'glorifies the religion of the smile, and insists that only by each separate soul surrendering to God can the world be liberated from oppression ... it soon finds itself landed in the Fascist Camp'.[72] Perhaps somewhat tastelessly he remarked: 'If one concentrates one's love on "Jesus only" it may end by the consignment of one's neighbour to the concentration camp for the good of the Father-land.'[73] Similarly, the Arians, that party of 'court flunkeys and flatterers', also 'believed in God as a solitary tyrant in a far-away heaven, too great to come down and sojourn with man' who was 'best represented on earth by a solitary and all-powerful Emperor; whose will none might question'.[74]

In like manner, he suggests in his *Autobiography* that the Papist emphasis on transcendence rather than immanence has led the Church of Rome to Fascist conclusions: 'God the omnipotent Dictator in the Heavens is best represented by omnipotent dictators in Church and State, in infallible Popes and almighty *Führers*.'[75] For Noel this was the heresy which denied the immanence of the indwelling Word. Too much transcendence was always liable to distort the gospel since, according to Noel, 'God above is always thrusting Himself afresh into the world below and renewing the face of the earth'.[76] He is similarly critical of versions of socialism that emphasise the future at the expense of the present: the cry of 'When the revolution comes' could never excuse immorality in the here and now.[77] The immanence of catholicism could rescue socialists from their imprisonment within social forces and abstractions.

It was because true catholicism stressed the incarnation and material nature of God that good socialists were required to be catholics, since

> ... we believe that in the worship of the Communal God, the Trinity in Unity 'in which none is afore or after other, none is greater or less than another'; in the common meal of the Mass; in the worship of the Saints, champions

most of them of the people's rights and liberties, we gain an inspiration which cannot be gained by appeal to abstractions.[78]

The Mass, the fellowship meal of the kingdom, was stressed because of its material nature as well as its corporate dimension. It became the 'stirrup-cup to far-off victory' as the 'Fellowship of the Holy Meal':[79]

> The Mass ... is the manifestation of an all-pervading God in a common act and through material things, rather than the bringing down of an absent God into alien matter, so that as the drama of the eucharist unfolds itself, Christ is more and more manifest among us. This, then, is the 'Magic of the Mass'.[80]

Noel's *credo* was expressed in the epilogue to *Jesus the Heretic* in terms of a power of community which stemmed from a God who was himself community; it was the task of Christians to re-create a world in which there was an 'interplay of initiative and co-operation'.[81] God too had created beauty and dwelt in our world to liberate the oppressed and create the 'Commonwealth of God', an indwelling that was met with 'malice of the mighty masters of the world who dragged Him down to His Passion and Death on the Cross'.[82] The Church lived as the first-fruits of the kingdom as it sought 'to redeem mankind from the inward tyrannies of sin and the outward tyrannies of cruel men'.[83] In short, he went on: 'We, therefore, believe that our principal work is not "social reform" nor pietistic exercises, but the stirring within people of the hunger and thirst for righteousness which shall fill them with the eternal things and a due measure of things that are temporal.'[84]

Finally, it is worth looking briefly at Noel's view of Jesus, whom he discussed at length in *The Life of Jesus* published in 1939.[85] Though the book is far from original, and is over-long and erratic, it nevertheless portrays Jesus in relation to the politics of his day. Jesus, perhaps unsurprisingly, is understood as a great leader who directs people towards building the New World Order on earth, the kingdom of God. He sees it as the 'kingdom of justice and comradeship',[86] which is

> a world which Christ wishes to build here on earth. Although it is not to be a man-made kingdom, for it is God-planned and God-given, yet it must be man-accepted and man-actualized by the grace of God. No one now seriously contends that the constant 'this world' and 'the next world' of the gospels refers to the world in which we now live as contrasted with a world beyond the grave, but to 'this present age' contrasted with the 'age to come'.[87]

The kingdom of God required a complete reversal of economic relationships in

> . . . a company which was already becoming the

nucleus of the new world. If they were to estab-
lish the divine commonwealth on the foundation
of God's justice, if a world of men were to spring
up in which greed had given place to generosity
and domination to service, in which men co-
operated to produce, instead of competing to
destroy, all things would be added to them.[88]

It was on the basis of Jesus' attack on riches that
Noel develops his co-operative ethics, which, he
claims, is 'a thousand times truer to-day' than it
was in Jesus' own time. 'Under modern conditions,'
he goes on, 'the world has become so prolific that
if mankind were to take the Sermon on the Mount
seriously, the wants of every nation, and of all its
citizens, could be abundantly secured.'[89]

Noel's Jesus, however, is far from consistent.
Sometimes he is a revolutionary who will destroy
the present order with a cataclysmic event, and yet
at other times (and more often) the thrust of his
message is to entrust human beings with the
responsibility to destroy and rebuild. Nevertheless,
Jesus embodies a 'collective hope' which expresses
the kingdom of God, that kingdom which is to be
'built upon the eternal impulses of the whole
human race'.[90] Although its fullness rests in the
world beyond, it is nevertheless necessary to
attempt to construct this classless and co-operative
system in the present. Near the end of the book
Noel emphasises his strongly materialist Christ-
ology and his universalism:

If the [new commandment to love one another] be the revelation of one who was in the world from the beginning, in whom we live and move and have our being, it may be hard to obey; sin and stupidity may keep us from that obedience, and it may be with infinite difficulty that we find the way home. But it will be home to which at last we come. In commonwealth we shall have found him who is our life, and who has written his laws in our hearts, and we shall be travelling back by his grace into our proper nature as revealed in him. For mankind was made by him to be the Body of God.[91]

The human approach to God was thus 'through the representative man, and through the love of the brethren. Jesus reveals the essential nature of God and of man, his child and care, as comradeship, as love, as commonwealth'.[92] In short, commonwealth, fraternity and love are all incarnate in the man, Jesus Christ, who becomes our pattern and redeemer.

7. Conclusion

Soon after the publication of his book on Jesus, however, Noel's diabetes grew worse and he became increasingly frail and blind, dying eventually of cancer on 22 July 1942. At the end he remained the same 'gay, courageous rebel he had always been'.[93] In assessing the legacy of this extraordinary life, it can hardly be denied that Conrad Noel left his mark on the Church: he was undoubtedly a maverick and a romantic, and yet his sense of democracy and co-operation, as well as his sense of fun and joy, shaped an approach to church and society which was firmly rooted in the breadth of the catholic tradition but which was never exclusivist or elitist. Thaxted became famous for the quality, beauty and fun of its worship which sought to meet the challenge of sharing in a redeemed human community based on values of equality, participation and fraternity. Not surprisingly, there were many fond appreciations in a whole range of socialist and church magazines: the Archbishop of Canterbury, William Temple, for instance, thanked God for Noel's 'life of devoted and effective witness to the fullness of Christian truth'. The obituarist in *The Church Militant* noted that 'for Conrad Noel, the social and the individual aspects of Christian life were bound up with one another and were quite inseparable'.[94]

To add my own judgement to this, it seems to me that Noel was a genuine visionary, and although his practical solutions may have neglected some or even most of the complexities of realpolitik, he nevertheless sought to make the church an expression of the kingdom of righteousness, justice and equality and thus a beacon in a desperate world. The church was not merely a preacher of social justice – it was an experiment in community in which liturgy, life and beauty were all united. It took an eccentric to realise this vision and no doubt there was a snobbishness and a luddite romanticism which meant that the church remained detached from many of the workers.[95] Nevertheless in his warfare against the prosaic, Noel sought to integrate the particular and the universal, this world and the next in a new world order. Of course he failed – as all must fail – and yet he held on to the vision, dreaming the dreams for the world and trying to put them into practice. It is fruitful to compare Noel's vision with the half-hearted words of the editors of the *New English Hymnal*:

> It remains true that offering of objective praise and worship to God, the lover of mankind, is the ultimate ground of man's love of his fellow-men. By including a section headed 'the Kingdom of God' and similar hymns elsewhere in the book, we have not overlooked the social duty of Christ-

ians, but we believe that its application to immediate needs can often be better expressed in sermon and prayers than in hymnody.[96]

For those for whom beauty and duty formed an integrated whole, however, there could never be such a divorce between 'immediate needs' and the truths of the catholic faith: liturgy matters because the world matters and the world matters because liturgy matters. That is no dreary ecclesiasticism but a living form of life far removed from the emotional (and often deeply tasteless) excess of so much contemporary worship.

As is displayed by his almost mystical attachment to the wearing of sandals,[97] Noel conveyed the same air of aristocratic iconoclasm as St Francis and some of his beloved heroes. It was in this eccentric way that Noel managed to place Thaxted on the map as a place devoted to the celebration of English church life and cultural life. Noel's vision, however, was far from exclusivist (even if at times he was far from ecumenically-minded), always reaching out beyond national boundaries towards the greater democracy embodied in the variety and diversity of churches and nations and symbolised by international socialism and the catholic faith. It was undoubtedly true that such a catholic vision could only survive in small counter-cultural groups, but such groups have provided a momentum which has spread out far beyond Thaxted and the Church of England.[98] Indeed, one could claim that there is much to recommend Noel's vision of harmony which rebelled against a world of monotony. For this reason I will finish with Noel's ecumenical and internationalist vision of the Church of the future included in H.G. Wells's collection, *The Great State*:

> Within the Church itself ... there exists a great variety of ideas and a great variety of worship. There are to be found within its organization many companies whose members before the great changes were dissenters; each has its shrine or oratory, and emphasises some one or other aspect of the truth, but without breaking away in thought or emotion (heresy) or in organization (schism) from the bond and proportion of the Catholic religion ... the common worship of the Church is elaborate, for it is the people's tribute to the Supreme Ritualist who is making a rich and complex and visible world with its pageantry of days and nights, and of the varying seasons. But to many of the guilds the ceremonial makes no special appeal.[99]

This is a fundamentally Maurician vision of catholicity which points to the democracy of all people created in God's image, an image of unity in variety expressed in materiality and sacramentality. And the alternative to such a vision, according to Noel, led to evil, which

> ... is that which injures community ... In an anti-social age everything from religion to busi-

ness had become distorted, neurotic, excessively introspective, but now the sacraments were again the witnesses and effectual signs of social grace.[100]

In our contemporary mix-and-match world of the *Visual Liturgy* there is every likelihood that the sacraments, hymns and everything else that goes on in church will become just as ephemeral as the reams of A4 paper produced by the parish photocopier: liturgy divorced from life makes the church into an ever more esoteric social club. But without a living liturgy what hope is there that the sermon will serve the 'immediate needs' of a world crying out for justice? Who will be there to hear it? Noel's vision is of what it might be to transform the world through our worship, to make it that place where God can reign and where alleluias might be sung – and danced – from every village. It is about beauty, truth and justice. Those are the values which should shape our liturgy, our hymns and our life. And our service to the world is to banish ugliness, lies and injustice through living a New World Order. Life, liturgy and socialism live or die together. One can but hope that contemporary Anglican catholics remember this before it is too late.

Notes

1. C.E. Raven, *Christian Socialism, 1848–1854* (London: Macmillan, 1920), pp. 20–1.
2. Peter d'A Jones, *The Christian Socialist Revival, 1877–1914*, Part Two (Princeton: Princeton University Press, 1968). Cf. Donald Gray, *Earth and Altar: the Evolution of the Parish Communion in the Church of England to 1945*, Part Two (Norwich: Canterbury Press, Alcuin Club, 1986).
3. Percy Dearmer, *The Parson's Handbook* (1899), seventh edn (London: Oxford University Press, 1909), 'Introductory essay on conformity to the Church of England', pp. 4f.
4. Cited in Reg Groves, *Conrad Noel and the Thaxted Movement. An Adventure in Christian Socialism* (New York: Augustus M. Keeley, 1968), p. 219. On Noel, see also Maurice B. Reckitt, *Maurice to Temple* (London: Faber and Faber, 1947), Chapter V and VI; Robert Woodifield, 'Conrad Noel' in *For Christ and People*, ed. Maurice B. Reckitt (London: SPCK, 1968); E.R. Norman, *Church and Society in England 1770–1970. A Historical Study* (Oxford: Clarendon Press, 1976); Mark Arman, *Conrad, Miriam, Jack and Barbara* (Thaxted: Workshop Press, 1992); Chris Bryant, *Possible Dreams. A Personal History of Christian Socialists* (London: Hodder and Stoughton, 1996), Chapter 5; Alan Wilkinson, *Christian Socialism: Scott Holland to Tony Blair* (London: SCM Press Ltd, 1998), esp. pp. 163–5.
5. *Jesus the Heretic* (London: J.M. Dent, 1939), p. 37.
6. *The Life of Jesus* (London: J.M. Dent, 1937), p. xiii.
7. *Socialism in Church History* (London: Frank Palmer, 1910), p. 245. Robert Woodifield remarked in an obituary that Noel drew most from Maurice, and like him, was a 'liberal humanist democratic Catholic'.
8. *Byways of Belief* (London: Frank Palmer, 1912), pp. 27f.

9. *An Autobiography*, ed. Sydney Dark (London: J.M. Dent, 1945), p. 33.

10. Cf. Nan Dearmer, *The Life of Percy Dearmer* (London: Jonathan Cape, 1940), pp. 90f. Percy Widdrington later paid this tribute to Noel: 'No priest in the country could claim so wide a knowledge of the Labour movement . . .His lectures and debates created a deep impression and a friendliness which did much to remove the suspicion in Labour circles that the Church was hostile.' Cited in M.B. Reckitt, *Faith and Society* (London: Longmans, 1932), p. 107.

11. On this, see Graham Neville, *Radical Churchman. Edward Lee Hicks and the New Liberalism* (Oxford: Clarendon, 1998), p. 116.

12. On this, see Jones, *The Christian Socialist Revival*, Chapter 5.

13. *Byways of Belief*, p. 231.

14. Neville, *Radical Churchman*, p. 116. Hicks gave Noel's first book, *Socialism in Church History*, a particularly scathing review in the *Manchester Guardian* (cf. p. 277).

15. *Autobiography*, p. 59.

16. *Autobiography*, p. 57.

17. In the last paragraph of his introduction to the *English Hymnal*, Dearmer wrote: 'the best hymns of Christendom are as free as the Bible from the self-centred sentimentalism, the weakness and unreality which mark inferior productions. The great hymns, indeed, of all ages abound in the conviction that duty lies at the heart of the Christian life – a double duty to God and to our neighbour; and such hymns, like the Prayer Book, are for all sorts and conditions of men.'

18. *Autobiography*, p. viii.

19. On the Church Socialist League, see Jones, *The Christian Socialist Revival*, Chapter 7.

20. *Autobiography*, p. 60.

21. *Church Socialist*, Vol. I, no. 1 (1912).

22. *Jesus the Heretic*, p. 34.

23. *Jesus the Heretic*, p. 35.

24. *The Life of Jesus*, p. xviii.

25. Cited in *The Life of Jesus*, p. xix.

26. *The Life of Jesus*, p. xix.
27. *The Life of Jesus*, p. 538.
28. However, it must be admitted that, like Hewlett Thompson, Noel was somewhat over-enthusiastic about Stalin's Russia. See *The Life of Jesus*, p. 541.
29. Norman, *Church and Society in England 1770–1970*, p. 248. Norman is wrong in claiming that Noel flew the red flag from the tower of the church. It was placed against the chancel arch.
30. *Socialism in Church History*, p. 257.
31. *Socialism in Church History*, p. 29.
32. *Socialism in Church History*, p. 7.
33. *Socialism in Church History*, p. 279.
34. *Socialism in Church History*, p. 282. Noel was, however, deeply critical of establishment variations of Anglicanism. At one point in *The Life of Jesus* he talks of the catholic doctrine of tyrannicide (p. 539), before claiming that 'The Anglican Church seems to have collapsed with the restoration of the monarchy and to have reached its deepest depravity about the middle of the Victorian era' (p. 540).
35. *Autobiography*, p. 91.
36. *The Life of Jesus*, p. 534.
37. John Milbank, 'Socialism of the Gift, Socialism by Grace', *New Blackfriars* 77 (1996), p. 544.
38. Cited in Paul T. Phillips, *A Kingdom on Earth. Anglo-American Social Christianity. 1880–1940* (University Park: Pennsylvania State University Press, 1996), p. 153.
39. Cited in Groves, *Conrad Noel*, p. 223.
40. *Byways of Belief*, p. 232.
41. Cited in Groves, *Conrad Noel*, p. 74.
42. *Autobiography*, p. 125.
43. *The Life of Jesus*, p. 536.
44. Jack Putterill, *Thaxted Quest for Social Justice. The Autobiography of Fr Jack Putterill – Turbulent Priest and Rebel* (Marlow: Precision Press, 1977), p. 23.
45. *The Battle of the Flags. A Study in Christian Politics* (London: The Labour Publishing House, 1922), p. 7.
46. Cited in Groves, *Conrad Noel*, pp. 207f.
47. Cited in Groves, *Conrad Noel*, p. 254.
48. Cited in Donald Gray, *Earth and Altar*, p. 105.

49. *The Battle of the Flags*, p. 10.
50. *The Battle of the Flags*, p. 14.
51. *The Battle of the Flags*, p. 15.
52. *Autobiography*, p. 116.
53. *The Battle of the Flags*, p. 17.
54. *The Battle of the Flags*, p. 27.
55. *The Battle of the Flags*, p. 28. Later, Noel became far more critical of Sinn Fein, comparing it to some of the sectarian nationalists of the first century. ' "Ourselves" is the true translation of "Sinn Fein," but "Ourselves Alone" is the more fitting description of a section, not only in Ireland, but in most nationalist movements, who concentrate only on nationalist independence and forget interdependence which is its complement' (*The Life of Jesus*, p. 285).
56. *The Battle of the Flags*, p. 56.
57. *Jesus the Heretic*, p. 184.
58. *The Battle of the Flags*, p. 66.
59. *The Battle of the Flags*, p. 93.
60. *Jesus the Heretic*, p. 197.
61. *Jesus the Heretic*, p. 205.
62. *Jesus the Heretic*, p. 205.
63. *Jesus the Heretic*, p. 207.
64. *Jesus the Heretic*, p. 46.
65. *The Battle of the Flags*, p. 56.
66. *The Battle of the Flags*, p. 95.
67. *Byways of Belief*, p. 277.
68. *Jesus the Heretic*, p. 179.
69. *Jesus the Heretic*, p. 2.
70. *The Battle of the Flags*, p. 95.
71. *The Battle of the Flags*, p. 95.
72. *Jesus the Heretic*, p. 12.
73. *Jesus the Heretic*, p. 14.
74. *The Battle of the Flags*, p. 95.
75. *Jesus the Heretic*, p. 37.
76. *Jesus the Heretic*, p. 31.
77. *Jesus the Heretic*, p. 30.
78. *Jesus the Heretic*, p. 46.
79. *Jesus the Heretic*, p. 211.
80. *Jesus the Heretic*, p. 218.
81. *Jesus the Heretic*, p. 219.

82. *Jesus the Heretic*, p. 220.
83. *Jesus the Heretic*, p. 221.
84. *Jesus the Heretic*, p. 221.
85. For a somewhat unfavourable appraisal of Noel's understanding of Jesus, see Ernst Bammel, 'The Revolution theory from Reimarus to Brandon' in *Jesus and the Politics of His Day*, ed. Ernst Bammel and C.F.D. Moule (Cambridge: Cambridge University Press, 1985), p. 57.
86. *The Life of Jesus*, p. 212.
87. *The Life of Jesus*, p. 580.
88. *The Life of Jesus*, p. 346.
89. *The Life of Jesus*, p. 346.
90. *The Life of Jesus*, p. 312.
91. *The Life of Jesus*, p. 588.
92. *The Life of Jesus*, p. 587.
93. Groves, *Conrad Noel*, p. 324.
94. *The Church Militant* 63 (1941), p. 3.
95. Alan Wilkinson thus asks: 'Noel created a remarkably beautiful church and liturgy at Thaxted and a community which attracted as many from outside as inside the parish. But did it attract the farm workers?' (*Christian Socialism*, p. 164).
96. *New English Hymnal* (Norwich: Canterbury Press, 1986), p. vi.
97. *Autobiography*, p. viii.
98. *Jesus the Heretic*, p. 211.
99. Cited in *Autobiography*, p. 92.
100. Cited in *Autobiography*, p. 92.